THE SECRET THOUGHTS OF

HORSES

THE SECRET THOUGHTS
OF
HORSES

BY
CJ Rose

THE
collective
BOOK STUDIO

Whup, I almost just stepped right in that dog doo-doo! Who just poops on the ground and leaves it there?

On three, we dump these spoiled brats and blow this popsicle stand!

Something I can help you with back there, pal?

If I were a
My Little Pony,
my name would be
Twilight Sparkle.
What about you?

Oh yeah, that's the spot.

Photobomb!
Put that in your
stinking album!

I hope this is the last Renaissance Faire of the year. The reek of human dorkiness is almost intolerable.

I am having the hardest time figuring out this yoga position.

This is officially the height of humiliation.

I love you
forever and ever.

Nothing says "Happy Holidays" like a scratchy fake wreath and an agitated cat.

I am just getting started with you, cowpoke!!!

I am literally poetry in motion.

When do you think
the hairless ape
will show up with
the grub?

Okay, the cute
new mare is heading
this way. Try to
look casual.

Theoretically, I could be a hornless unicorn. I'm going to roll with that.

Yes, you two may
be a little faster,
but I have the
gorgeous blonde mane,
so I win regardless.

My agent is *so* fired after we wrap this ridiculous photoshoot.

Okay, I agree. It is a pretty nice view. But, he didn't have to do any of the work to get us up here!

Why do we have to
belong to the only
farmer in town
too cheap to buy
a tractor?

If this horn were real, I would use it to gore the moron who dyed my mane and tail pink.

I feel like my perm is starting to wear off.

**Sorry, Frosty,
but you should
have gone with
the button nose.**

Eat my dust,
Black Beauty!

I think I ate too much of that funny-smelling plant the farmer's son secretly grows.

OMG, I totally startled myself with the sound of my own fart!

Hand over the carrots, or this could get ugly.

Someone move this kid closer to me!

I once had an audition as a spokeshorse for a famous beer company. But, after taste-testing their products, it was a no-go for me!

Dude, I think it might be time to get yourself a wee bigger horse before you break my spine.

I agree that the falling tree would make a sound, even if we weren't there to hear it. I love our existential discussions, Mr. Paws.

Can I have just a few more of those oats?

I know I'm not big, but I am irresistibly fluffy. Would you like to cuddle?

Come back in a week, and this thing will be gone.

Alright, you caught me. So I like to give the goat pony rides. I own that.

If you say I look like Rod Stewart, I will bite you.

I knew that I totally should have brought my skimboard today.

Whisper all the sweet nothings that you want. . . . I still like your wife better.

Hey, did you happen to see three hobbits around here?

Come hither and have a delightful roll in the grass with me.

I'm not saying there is anything wrong with your chick lit, but how about a good western?

I should never
have agreed to a
staring contest with
this dog. In the snow,
of all places!

What do you call
a horse that likes
to stay up late?
A night mare!

Who needs
peripheral vision
when you have such
a ravishing mane?

Why is this ridiculous human attempting a mind meld on me? Just go do a three-day yoga retreat/juice fast with your New Age friends and leave me alone!

I agree with you.
This is definitely the
dumbest sport the
humans have come up
with yet.

OMG, that mare over there is so jelly of my bling.

Look deeply into my eye, human, and slowly put that bit into your *own* mouth. That's it.

Is that the hay
delivery guy
we're hearing??

I know her perfume smells gross, but just pretend to like her and eventually she'll dole out the sugar cubes.

Yodel-ay-hee-hee-hoo!!!!

Hey, Ma, wait for me!

I am almost done
nuzzling him.
Then you guys can
have a turn.

I love you, too,
little ape lady.

Library of Congress catalog in Publication data is available.

ISBN: 978-1-68555-164-3
Ebook ISBN: 978-1-68555-966-3
LCCN: 2023930414

Printed and bound in China by
Reliance Printing Company Limited, Shenzhen.

Printed using Forest Stewardship Council certified stock
from sustainably managed forests.

Cover and interior design by AJ Hansen.
All images courtesy of Shutterstock.

1 3 5 7 9 10 8 6 4 2

The Collective Book Studio®
Oakland, California
www.thecollectivebook.studio